COME BACK, SALMON

HOW A GROUP OF DEDICATED KIDS ADOPTED PIGEON CREEK AND BROUGHT IT BACK TO LIFE ✄

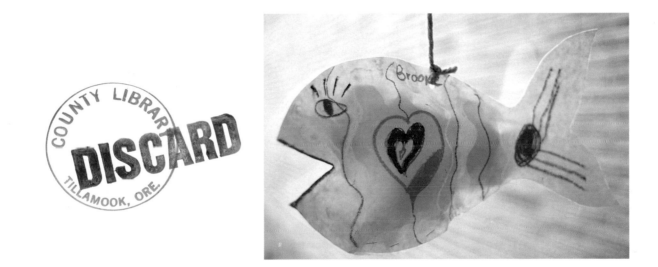

by Molly Cone ✄ Photographs by Sidnee Wheelwright

Sierra Club Books for Children
San Francisco

To kids everywhere who are
making a difference

The Sierra Club, founded in 1892 by John Muir, has devoted itself to the study and protection of the earth's scenic and ecological resources—mountains, wetlands, woodlands, wild shores and rivers, deserts and plains. The publishing program of the Sierra Club offers books to the public as a nonprofit educational service in the hope that they may enlarge the public's understanding of the Club's basic concerns. The Sierra Club has some sixty chapters in the United States and in Canada. For information about how you may participate in its programs to preserve wilderness and the quality of life, please address inquiries to Sierra Club, 730 Polk Street, San Francisco, CA 94109.

Library of Congress Cataloging-in-Publication Data

Cone, Molly.
    Come back, salmon/by Molly Cone; photographs by Sidnee Wheelwright. — 1st ed.
      p.   cm.
    Includes index.
    Summary: Describes the efforts of the Jackson Elementary School in Everett, Washington, to clean up a nearby stream, stock it with salmon, and preserve it as an unpolluted place where the salmon could return to spawn.
    ISBN 0-87156-572-2
    1. Fish habitat improvement—Washington (State)—Pigeon Creek—Citizen participation—Juvenile literature. 2. Coho salmon—Washington (State)—Pigeon Creek—Juvenile literature. 3. Jackson Elementary School (Everett, Wash.)—Juvenile literature. 4. Pacific salmon—Juvenile literature. [1. Fish habitat improvement. 2. Salmon. 3. Environmental protection. 4. Jackson Elementary School (Everett, Wash.)] I. Wheelwright, Sidnee, ill. II. Title.
SH157.8.C66   1991
639.3'755—dc20   91-29023

Book and jacket design: Bonnie Smetts
Illustrations: Rik Olson
Printed in Hong Kong
10 9 8 7 6 5 4 3 2 1

ACKNOWLEDGMENTS

The Jackson Elementary School stream restoration project was inspired by a Washington State Environmental Education seminar led by Snohomish County Adopt-A-Stream Foundation director Tom Murdoch. The seminar was attended by Jackson School teachers Vicki Hill and Laurie Baker.

The author and photographer wish to thank the teachers and students of Jackson School for their help and cooperation in translating their experiences into this book. Special thanks are due Brandon King and Vicki Hill for their extraordinary help, interest, and attention during the writing and photographing of this book. Thanks also to Laurie Baker and to teachers Doug Forrey, Pat Johnston, and Rita Husby; to principal Linda Fisher; to staff members Marilyn Whitford, Bobbie Stencil, and Sherry McGilvray; and to the Jackson School PTA.

The dialogue in this book is based on interviews with the children and teachers of Jackson Elementary School, taped by the author and photographer.

Special thanks from the author to Dr. Kenneth A. Henry, Fishery Biologist (Research) of NOAA, National Marine Fisheries Service, Alaska Fisheries Center; to Joan Berryman, Roy Metzgar, and Daniel J. Mathias of the City of Everett Public Works Department; and to K.C. Wheelwright for his reading of the manuscript and his suggestions from a student's viewpoint.

Special thanks from the photographer to Chris Huss and also to Lloyd Weller, Thomas Russo, and Jim Nilsen for photographic assistance; to Larry Telles of the Quilcene National Fish Hatchery; and to Don Rudnick and John Munn at the Skykomish State Salmon Hatchery.

CONTENTS

CHAPTER 1

WHERE DID ALL THE SALMON GO?

Pigeon Creek #1 flows for about two miles. From the southwestern edge of the city of Everett, Washington, it makes its way north to Puget Sound. Its last half-mile runs just below Jackson Elementary School. To get to the Sound, the creek flows through a culvert, or large pipe, under the railroad tracks and then across a sandy beach.

FISH HAD DISAPPEARED FROM JUNK-FILLED PIGEON CREEK. ⤙

None of the students at Jackson School had ever seen a fish in Pigeon Creek. What the fifth graders saw in the creek when they followed the wooded trail down from their school grounds on a sunny fall day in 1984 was muddy water. Scattered through it were bottles and cans, squashed Styrofoam cups, torn six-pack holders, old tires, and a lot of other junk. Along the banks were a broken-down refrigerator, a set of bedsprings, and some smashed cardboard cartons.

The students in Mr. King's fifth grade class stood there looking at all the trash, making faces.

"Yuck! What is this, anyway?"

"It looks like a garbage dump to me."

"No," said Mr. King. "It's a stream. It was a clear, clean stream when I was a little boy. It was named Pigeon Creek because of all the pigeons nesting around here."

The members of the class stared at their teacher. They couldn't imagine him ever being a little boy, any more than they could imagine this muddy, trash-filled gully ever being a stream.

"I don't see any pigeons."

"I don't see much of a creek, either."

"Hey! I see water moving right there — under those old tires."

"Salmon used to be born in Pigeon Creek," Mr. King told them. "They'd hatch from eggs laid on the gravelly bottom, and they'd swim around until they were big enough to migrate to the Pacific Ocean. Then, after they stayed in the ocean awhile, they'd come back again. There's one thing to remember about salmon — they always return to their home stream to spawn."

"*Spawn?*"

"He means make babies."

Mr. King was still gazing at all the rubble. "Once Pigeon Creek was full of spawning salmon. In the ocean, they were sleek and silvery. But salmon change color when they're ready to mate. As they'd come swimming upstream, their sides would turn red."

"Hey! Can we go over to the beach for a while?"

"I can remember," Mr. King continued in a far-off voice, "when Pigeon Creek ran red with salmon."

The fifth graders stared at the muddy, clogged stream. It was hard to believe that Pigeon Creek had ever been filled with water flowing free and clear, let alone had fish swimming in it.

In the time it had taken their teacher to grow from a little boy to an adult, other changes had taken place as well. Everett, Washington, had grown from a medium-size town to a flourishing city. As in fast-growing cities everywhere,

more people meant more houses, more shopping centers, more streets, and more parking lots.

As neighborhoods grew, more trees were taken down and more land was cleared. When it rained, soft soil slid down the bare hillsides. When dirt was moved, it was often dumped close to a stream or even into it. No one paid much attention when a tiny and seemingly unimportant creek got filled with dirt or buried underground.

As more families filled more houses, grass cuttings and litter were often tossed into the nearest creek, gully, or ravine. Old oil from cars and sudsy water

THE RUBBISH THAT PEOPLE HAD THROWN AWAY HADN'T GONE AWAY. ⌐

FIFTH GRADERS SCRAMBLED OVER THE ROCKS WHERE PIGEON CREEK FLOWED THROUGH A CULVERT INTO PUGET SOUND. ⤙

from car washings flowed down the nearest street drain into the streams. The fertilizers that made lawns greener and the pesticides that killed garden bugs also went down the drains and into the streams, carried by the rain.

Gradually the clear water of nearby streams and creeks turned brown and murky. Gradually the fish disappeared. And before anyone knew it, creeks and streams like Pigeon Creek no longer ran red with salmon.

The fifth graders quickly moved away from the creek that had lain neglected and forgotten for so many years. On the beach nearby, they hollered and shrieked, chasing each other across the sand. They scrambled over big rocks and hunted for baby crabs at the water's edge.

Few gave the abandoned stream another thought until the day the principal made an announcement: Jackson Elementary School was going to adopt Pigeon Creek.

Adopt a stream? Suddenly everybody was talking about it. How were they supposed to adopt a stream?

"My aunt just adopted a baby. Every time I go over there, she's feeding it or bathing it or changing its diaper."

"Well, sure. If you adopt a baby, you've got to take care of it."

"Our old dog adopted a kitten. She growls when anyone even comes near it."

The Jackson School teachers told their classes that adopting a stream meant giving it the care and attention it needed. They would clean it up, stock it with fish raised from eggs in a classroom aquarium, and bring the salmon back.

The first and second graders listened in wonder. The third and fourth graders opened their eyes wide and said, "You mean *us?*" But few of Mr. King's fifth graders said anything at all. They didn't think any kind of fish would ever live in Pigeon Creek again.

SURPRISING DISCOVERIES WERE MADE ALONG THE SHORE.

CHAPTER 2 ⊷

OPERATION PIGEON CREEK

EVERY FIFTH GRADER PITCHED IN TO CLEAN UP THE ADOPTED STREAM. ⊷

Trailing along behind their teachers, Mr. King and Mr. Baker, Jackson School's two classes of fifth graders headed down the winding path to Pigeon Creek. Armed with garbage sacks, they scattered like seabirds to pluck the litter from the banks of the stream.

When older students from nearby Evergreen Middle School arrived in a truck and jumped out to help, everybody suddenly began working a little harder.

Into large plastic garbage sacks went candy wrappers, old shoes, glass bottles, aluminum cans, pizza boxes, Styrofoam cups, scraps of paper, broken toys, and six-pack holders. From the middle of the creek were pulled rusty car parts, bent oil cans, a "For Sale" sign, mattresses and old bedsprings, a broken-down chair, and lots of old tires.

The pile of garbage on the roadway grew so high that it took many truckloads to haul it all away. In the following weeks, every Jackson School class took turns helping with the cleanup.

"Whew! This is hard work!"

"Well, think of it this way," said Mr. Baker. "We're not hauling trash, we're bringing a stream back to life."

STUDENTS PULLED TOGETHER TO
REMOVE THE JUNK. ᐧ

SILT SPELLS DANGER TO FISH. ⌐

Some of the people who lived nearby weren't exactly encouraging about Jackson School's Pigeon Creek project.

"You're wasting your time," said one. "Bringing salmon back to Pigeon Creek is nothing but a dream."

Mr. King told his class, "To accomplish anything, you have to have a dream. Everything worthwhile starts with a dream."

For a while, it seemed as if the little creek would never stay free of trash. People came in their cars and trucks over the weekends to dump more. One school morning, the Jackson School students found 600 old tires dumped onto the banks of the stream. It wasn't easy to haul them out. The principal had to call in the city parks department to help. From then on, the fifth graders took turns patrolling the creek banks before and after school and on weekends to keep trash dumpers away.

The students soon learned that using gullies and ravines as trash dumps wasn't the only danger to fish life in a stream.

Just as dangerous was stripping hillsides bare of all their trees to build houses. When it rained, loose dirt slid down into the stream.

"This bottom is nice and soft," said a fifth grader, wading into Pigeon Creek. Ankle deep, he wiggled his bare toes into the powdery covering.

"The soft stuff is silt," Mr. King told his students. "It feels nice to us but not to the fish coming back to spawn. Salmon lay their eggs in gravel. But if the gravel is covered with silt, the eggs can't breathe — and they suffocate."

"Arrggghhhh!" said the wader, clutching the neckline of his T-shirt and staggering out of the water.

As Operation Pigeon Creek continued, words like *silt, watershed, environment,* and *pollution* became part of the everyday vocabulary of the 450 students in the red brick school on top of the hill.

They began to learn that other things were as threatening to fish life as silt.

"The worst thing you can do is dump your used oil and antifreeze, your insect killer, or anything with detergent in it down a storm drain," their teachers told them. "That is, if you want fish to live in the creek."

But there really was no *if* about it. Suddenly, what all the kids in Jackson School wanted more than anything was to see salmon come back to Pigeon Creek.

They stenciled DUMP NO WASTE — DRAINS TO STREAM signs on the storm drains leading to Pigeon Creek. They went around their neighborhoods knocking on doors to remind people that almost everything poured down the street drains ended up in the stream. They ran after walkers, joggers, and strollers to

STENCILED REMINDERS ON STORM DRAINS HELPED MAKE THE CREEK SAFE FOR FISH LIFE. ⌐

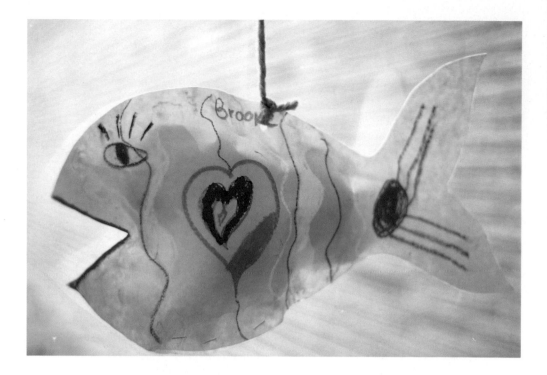

hand out leaflets asking people not to pollute the stream. The more they learned about their adopted creek, the harder they worked to keep it clean.

"Pigeon Creek is past saving," people kept telling them. "Maybe you should just forget it."

"How many of you want to forget it?" Mr. Baker asked his students one day. No one raised a hand. Mr. Baker grinned.

"If you have a dream, you can't let anyone take it away from you," Mr. King told his class.

The first and second graders drew pictures of fish, painted them, and hung them in the school windows. The third graders made crayon and poster-paint drawings and taped them in the hallways. The fourth and fifth graders combined art, science, writing, and research to create their own books on the life cycle of the salmon. In almost every class, including math and geography, students were doing something that connected up with Operation Pigeon Creek.

When the Port of Everett announced its plan to build a log storage facility at the mouth of Pigeon Creek, Jackson School students looked at each other in dismay.

"That'll block our stream!"

"What do they care? They don't even know about our Pigeon Creek project."

"We've got to tell them."

"Why would they listen to us? We're just kids."

"Even kids can make a difference."

"Who says?"

"Mr. King says. 'You can make a difference.' That's what he always says."

"Yeah."

TALES WERE TOLD AND IDEAS LAUNCHED IN MR. KING'S STORYBOAT. ❧

The fifth graders started writing letters — a lot of letters. They wrote to the port officials, the mayor of the city, the members of the city council, state and county officials, and the Everett *Herald,* the city's daily newspaper.

The Port of Everett officials were surprised to hear about the plans that the Jackson School students had for Pigeon Creek. The mayor and the city council members were surprised, too. The Everett *Herald* sent a reporter to the school to take a picture of the students and their adopted stream.

Because of the students' action, the port officials decided to build their storage facility someplace else. Sighing in relief, the fifth graders continued to stand guard over Pigeon Creek.

Gradually, people living nearby began to help the students keep the creek clean. A woman called the school one morning when she noticed that the creek was running muddy. A man who regularly walked his dog near the creek area began to pick up scattered candy wrappers and soft drink cans he found along the way. Joggers kept their eyes open for trash dumpers.

Operation Pigeon Creek was well on its way.

EVERETT CITY COUNCIL AND JACKSON STUDENTS WORKED TOGETHER TO SAVE PIGEON CREEK. ➤

CHAPTER 3

THE FISH THAT WENT TO SCHOOL

JANUARY

Everybody walking down the first floor hallway stopped to look into the new glass fish tank set into the wall. They could see right through it into Mrs. Hill's first grade classroom. It replaced the old plastic aquarium that had once held goldfish. A grant from Snohomish County had paid for the tank, an air pump, two small filters, and a cooling unit. School district science funds provided water-testing kits.

EVEN EMPTY, THE NEW FISH TANK ATTRACTED ATTENTION. ⬤

The new tank held eggs that would grow into baby Coho salmon to stock Pigeon Creek. More than a thousand of them had arrived from the Skykomish State Salmon Hatchery in a wet gunnysack inside a bucket. Now they lay in two wooden trays floating at the top of the water and in one metal tray set down on the bottom so the smaller children could see them.

Every class in the school took turns coming to look at the eggs in the tank. Peering into the trays, they saw row upon row of pearly, red, pea-size balls. On each egg were two tiny black dots.

"The black dots are eyes," Mr. King told his fifth graders. His students crowded together in front of the tank gazing at the eyed eggs.

"Hey! They're looking at us!"

"You mean those fish eggs can see?"

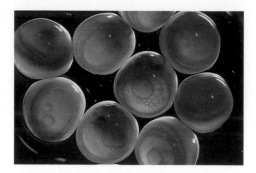

THE EYED EGG SPINS AROUND...

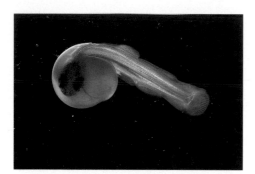

...UNTIL THE CASING BREAKS OPEN...

...AND THE ALEVIN BEGINS TO EMERGE. ⌖

"I guess if they have eyes they can see."

"Potatoes have eyes, and they can't see."

The eggs in the school fish tank were one month old. That's how old Coho salmon eggs are when the eyes appear. The eyes are the only part of the embryo growing inside the egg that can be seen from the outside.

In a stream, the eyed eggs would still have been under the gravel in their nest, or *redd.* "They still have a lot of developing to do before they become Coho salmon," Mr. King said.

The tiny embryos growing inside the eyed eggs needed cool water to survive. Stream water is naturally cold because it comes from melted snow, cold underground springs, or cool rain. For the eyed eggs in the schoolroom tank to stay alive and continue to grow, the water had to be kept as cool as the water in a stream.

The fifth graders learned how to test the temperature of the water in the tank. Every day, someone had to make sure it stayed at about 50 degrees Fahrenheit. When the water began to get too warm, a student turned on a mechanical cooling unit attached to the top of the tank.

The eyed eggs rested in the trays in the fish tank almost the same way they would have rested at the bottom of the stream, under the gravel in their redd. But the gravel in the stream protects the eggs and the sensitive embryos inside them from bright sunlight. In order to protect the eyed eggs in the school tank from the bright school lights, Mrs. Hill put a sheet of black plastic over the glass sides.

FEBRUARY

Three weeks after the eyed eggs arrived, excitement rippled through the halls of Jackson School like a breeze through a woodland. Something important was going on in the fish tank.

Clusters of children gathered on both sides of the tank, trying to see in.

"What's happening? What's happening?"

The eyed eggs were spinning around. White foam was rising around them.

"They're hatching," Mr. King said.

"He means they're getting born," someone told a first grader.

"Look! Some heads are wiggling out!"

"'Let me out! Let me out!'" a girl squeaked in a tiny voice. "That's what they're saying."

"I can't hear anything," said the first grader.

When an egg begins to hatch, the salmon embryo inside the egg starts spinning around so fast that the egg breaks open and the little newborn fish comes out. Soon the tank was full of twirling eggs and emerging fish.

But they didn't look like any kind of fish anyone in Jackson School had ever seen. They were tiny, fragile creatures with huge eyes, long, thin tails, and big orange bellies.

"Now they're *alevins*," said Mr. King. "That's what they're called when they hatch. *Al-e-vins*. The big orange belly is called a *yolk sac*. It holds all the nourishment an alevin needs until it is big enough to find food for itself."

A voice rose high. "My mother's not going to believe this! Wait 'til I tell her our fish hatched out with their own lunch sacks!"

Many of the parents couldn't believe that the eggs had hatched at all. Some of them came to school that afternoon to see for themselves.

The fifth graders eagerly taught the visitors what they had learned just that day. In the sac was a completely balanced diet of protein, carbohydrates, vitamins, and minerals. A threadlike tube running up through the center of the sac gave the alevin the oxygen it needed from the water.

As the eggs hatched, empty egg casings began to float through the water. Soon they were clogging the tank filters. As more and more alevins hatched, the filters in

LEAVING THE CASING BEHIND...

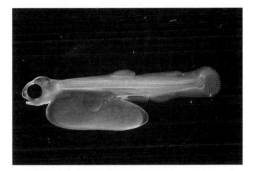

...THE ALEVIN FEEDS OFF ITS YOLK SAC...

...WHICH GETS SMALLER AND SMALLER AS THE ALEVIN GROWS. ⤙

A SALMON SLEEPS WITH ITS EYES OPEN

A salmon's eyes are open all the time, even when it is at rest. It can't close them, because it has no eyelids. It sees very well even when it's traveling at night or in deep water where there is not much light.

A salmon has an eye on each side of its head. They point in opposite directions and have a wide field of vision. This means that a salmon can see what is on both sides of it at the same time. It clearly sees what is far in front of it as well. However, the eyes are placed so far apart that anything very close to the salmon's face looks a little blurry.

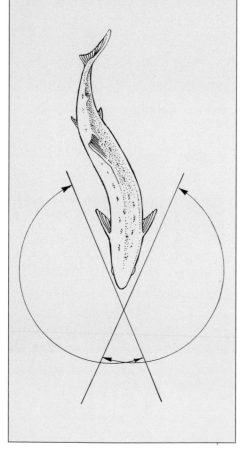

BLACK PLASTIC PROTECTED THE ALEVINS FROM BRIGHT LIGHTS AND TOO MANY VISITORS.

the tank had to be cleaned more and more often. At the same time, the crowds around the fish tank became larger and more frequent. Almost every student wanted to take a look at the alevins several times a day. Again and again, the black plastic was pushed away from the sides of the tank, letting the lights shine in. Hardly anybody noticed that the glass sides of the tank were uncovered most of the time — except the alevins.

They began to roll about clumsily, hampered by their big yolk sacs. They were seeking the darkness they would have had under the gravel in a stream. Trying to get away from the light, they scooted along the bottom of the tank, scraping their bellies. Not until the black plastic was pulled back into place did calm return to the inhabitants of the tank — and to the students of Jackson School.

Students now peered cautiously between the folds of the black plastic. They talked in whispers when they stopped in the hallway near the tank. The alevins were given the privacy they needed.

MARCH

A few weeks after the alevins hatched, the yolk sacs began to disappear. The alevins were "buttoning up." Their middles were becoming smooth and trim. The food in their sacs was almost completely used up.

In the stream, they would have been starting to wiggle out from under the gravel because they no longer had bulky yolk sacs holding them down. As soon as the alevins in the school tank buttoned up, the trays were taken out, the black plastic was removed, and the tank was full of tiny little fish swimming free. They were hardly more than one inch long.

"What do we call them now?" quizzed Mr. King.

"Fry!" shouted the fifth graders.

CHAPTER 4 ⊷

"GOOD-BYE, GOOD-BYE"

THE TINY NEW FISH DARTED ABOUT THE FISH TANK. ⊷

MARCH

The baby fish moved back and forth and up and down in the schoolroom tank. They swam by wiggling, using their tail fins to propel them and their side fins to balance and steer.

The scales that would soon cover them from head to tail like shining coats of armor were barely visible. A protective layer of slime glistened over the scales.

The fry breathed through their gills by opening and closing their mouths. When a fish opens its mouth, it is taking in water. When it closes its mouth, it is taking oxygen from the water that's running back out over its gills.

Enchanted with the tiny beings, the Jackson students could hardly bear to be away from the fish tank.

Like fry living in a stream, the fry in the school tank were not yet silver. They had dark bars, called *parr marks*, on their sides. In a stream, the parr marks help fry blend with the rocks so their enemies have a hard time seeing them.

"Hey, look! I stuck my finger in, and they're nibbling at it."

"That's because they're hungry," Mrs. Hill told her first graders. "They don't have their yolk sacs to lunch from anymore."

In a stream, the fry would have been feeding themselves by nibbling at katy-dids and other tiny bugs. At Jackson School, the fourth graders took turns feeding the fry in the tank. To begin with, a teaspoonful of fish food was sprinkled into the water twice a day. Then, two teaspoonsful.

The more the fry ate, the more they grew and the more crowded the tank became. Then some of the fry started to gulp for air at the surface of the water and roll upside down. Before anyone realized what was happening, a dead fry had floated down to the bottom of the tank.

HUNGRY FRY KNEW THAT THE SPOON MEANT FOOD. ←

WHAT ARE FINS FOR?

A salmon has seven fins that all work together to help the fish swim fast or slow and in the direction it wants to go.

The *tail fin,* or *caudal fin,* is like the rudder of a boat or airplane. It turns the fish right or left. It also acts as the fish's propeller, driving it forward. The two pairs of fins on each side of the fish's body — the *pectoral fins* and the *pelvic fins* — help it move up and down in the water. They also act as brakes to help the fish slow down or stop. The *back fin,* or *dorsal fin,* and the *anal fin* are used for balance. They keep the salmon from rolling over and over when it is moving through the water.

In addition to these seven fins, the salmon has a tiny, fleshy bump on its back, just in front of its tail. This is called the *adipose fin,* but its purpose is unknown. It could be called a family crest, because it is found only on members of the salmonid family.

DORSAL FIN   ADIPOSE FIN

PECTORAL FIN   PELVIC FIN   ANAL FIN   CAUDAL FIN

"What's wrong? Something's wrong!"

"Use the air pump!" the teacher said quickly. "They're not getting enough oxygen."

That is how the Jackson students learned that fry need plenty of oxygen to survive. From then on, the amount of oxygen in the tank was measured every day — and sometimes even twice a day.

APRIL

"Marta, can you tell us what exciting things are happening down in the fish tank today?"

"Well, the fish are swimming around."

"Are they eating much?"

"No."

"How can you tell they're not eating much?"

"There's food at the bottom."

"Are you sure that's food on the bottom?"

"Well, it looks like food."

"Does everybody agree?"

"Nah. Not me."

"Me neither. That's not food."

"What is it, then?"

"It's what's coming out the other end of the fish."

Everybody, even Marta, laughed.

But no one was laughing when the waste material on the bottom of the tank began to increase the amount of ammonia in the water. Too much ammonia takes the protective layer of slime off the fish. With the slime gone, mites can burrow under the scales and make the fish sick enough to die.

A flurry of concern flew through the school the day the ammonia in the water tested too high.

"Teacher says we have to take some of the water out and put new water in. And we have to do it fast."

"The way to do it is to take the end of a hose and suck on it to start the water flowing, then hurry up and put it in the bucket."

"Let me do it! I can do it!"

"Okay. Just suck on it, then put it in the bucket."

"Yeccch!"

A SAMPLE OF WATER WAS DIPPED UP DAILY FOR TESTING.

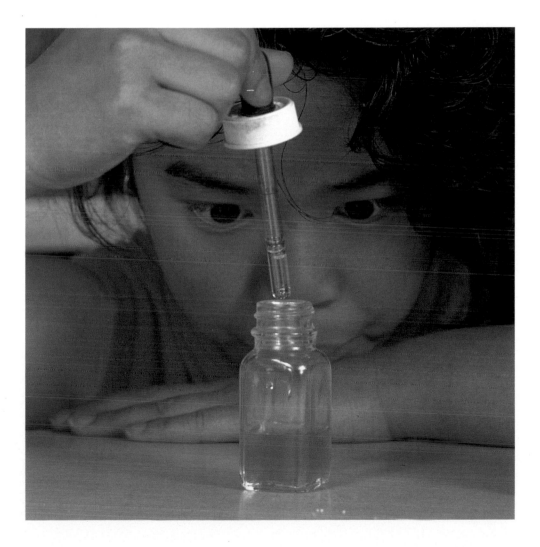

EVERY FIFTH GRADER LEARNED THE SKILL OF CAREFUL WATER TESTING.

TEST RESULTS CONFIRMED THAT THE TANK HAD ENOUGH OXYGEN TO KEEP THE FISH HEALTHY. ✒

"What's the matter?"

"I got a mouthful."

"You swallowed the water?"

He gulped. "I think I swallowed a fry."

Changing the water in the tank saved the fry that time, and many other times as well. Every student in school now knew the importance of oxygen and cool, clean water to the lives of the fish in the tank.

Testing the water in the fish tank became an important task for the fifth graders. Two by two, they took turns. Every morning when they got to school, they dipped a jar into the fish tank, trying not to get any fish in it, and carried it up to Mr. King's room. Taking out the testing kits, they filled each test tube with a sample of the water and added the required drops of chemicals.

When the oxygen in the water tested too low, oxygen had to be added to the tank with the air pump. When the ammonia in the water tested too high or when the acidity of the water wasn't right, the bottom of the tank had to be cleaned and the water in the tank changed.

MAY

Suddenly the tank seemed to be overflowing. The fry were now more than an inch and a half long and were jumping about. When the first graders walked into their room one morning, they found a high-leaping fry dead on the floor.

It was time to release the fry into the creek.

Early the next morning, the first graders watched as the fish in the school-room tank were transferred to plastic buckets filled with water and ice. With the ice keeping the water in the buckets cool and extra oxygen added with an air pump, the fry hardly seemed to notice the change. The buckets filled with fry were placed in a car and driven by a volunteer parent down to Pigeon Creek. Jumping and

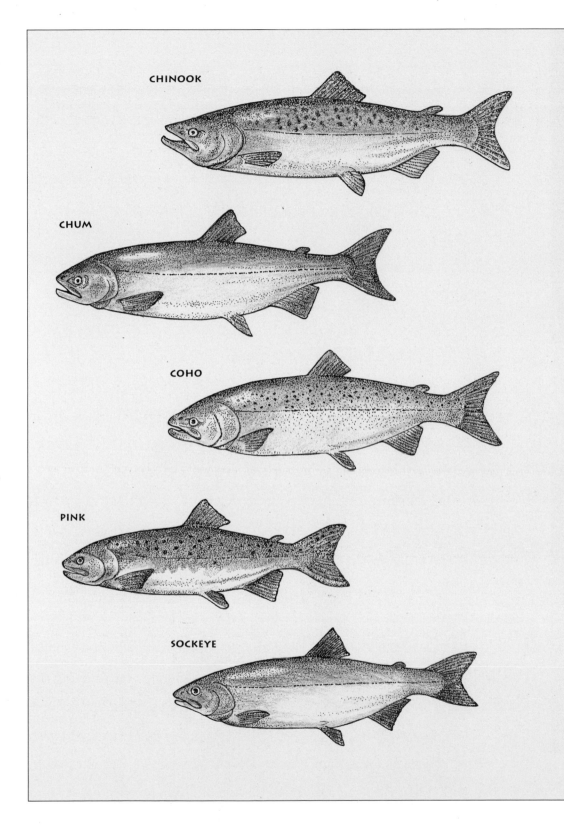

CHINOOK

CHUM

COHO

PINK

SOCKEYE

ALL IN THE FAMILY

All Pacific salmon are part of a family called *salmonids.* The scientific name for this family is *Salmonidae,* which comes from a Latin word meaning "the leaper."

Five kinds, or *species,* of salmon start life in the clear, flowing creeks and streams of the Pacific Northwest, migrate to the sea, and return to their home streams to spawn and to die. They are the *Chinook* (also called "King" or "Tyee," and sometimes called "Blackmouth" because of their black gums), the *Chum* (also called "Dog"), the *Coho* ("Silver"), the *Pink* ("Humpies"), and the *Sockeye* ("Red"). A sixth species, the *Steel-head,* returns to the sea again after spawning.

Pacific salmon have long, sleek bodies. In the ocean, their sides are silvery blue, their backs are blue-green, and their bellies are almost white. One way to tell the species apart is by the different speckles and spots on their tails and backs.

CLASS BY CLASS, EVERY JACKSON STUDENT RECEIVED AT LEAST ONE TINY COHO SALMON TO RELEASE INTO PIGEON CREEK. ⌖

THE LITTLE FISH WERE CAREFULLY TRANSFERRED FROM BUCKETS TO WATER-FILLED BAGS. ⌖

leaping themselves, the children hurried down the trail. They crowded around the buckets on the creek bank.

With a net, Mr. King scooped a fish into a little plastic bag filled with water. He handed a bag with a fish in it to each first grader. Mr. Baker helped some of the fifth graders scoop out the fish for themselves.

"Okay, now, each of you take your bag with your fish in it and carry it over to the creek," Mr. King instructed. "Tip the bag over the water and just let the fish spill out gently."

"I'm going to name mine first."

"So am I."

"Me too."

"My fish's name is Kathi, spelled with an *i*."

"Mine's Jayne, spelled with a *y*."

"Well, mine's Harlan Q. Hudpucker. And I'm not spelling it."

Standing on the bank, the Jackson School students watched the fry get used to their new home after the many weeks spent in the schoolroom tank.

Mr. King explained that, more than anything else, the fry would use their noses to get acquainted with the water. A fish has a keen sense of smell, and its nostrils are very sensitive to different odors in water. It would take young Harlan Q. Hudpucker and the other fry only about two weeks to memorize the particular smell of Pigeon Creek.

As long as the creek was kept clean and clear of pollution, Mr. King told the students, the fry would thrive and grow there for many months. Smelling the water, feeding, growing, and learning how to avoid anything that might swallow them whole, they would remain in the fresh water of the creek for as long as a year.

When the young Coho salmon were finally ready to leave Pigeon Creek to migrate to the sea, Mr. King explained, they would have grown from fry into

smolts. They'd be four to five inches long, with shiny, silvery coats, and they'd be ready to live in salt water. Traveling downstream tail-first, they would enter Puget Sound. Heading from there into the Straits of Juan de Fuca and out into the Pacific Ocean, they might even swim all the way to Alaska.

But no matter how far they went or how long they stayed away, Mr. King said, Pigeon Creek would remain deep in their memories all the rest of their lives.

"Goodbye, Jayne."

"Goodbye, Harlan Q. Hudpucker."

"Say hello to my Uncle George when you get to Juneau!"

"Remember to come back!"

FIRST GRADERS SAID GOOD-BYE TO THE FISH THEY HAD JUST NAMED. ❧

CHAPTER 5 ✦

THE JOURNEY

YEAR-OLD COHO SMOLT ARE READY TO MIGRATE TO THE OCEAN. ✦

A Pacific salmon's life begins and ends in the same freshwater stream, but during its lifetime it goes to the sea and back. It may swim thousands of miles in the time that it spends in the cold salt waters of the Pacific Ocean.

A young salmon starts its new life in the ocean by eating greedily. It spends its time diving for small sea creatures and feasting on the tiny drifting organisms called plankton. Feeding and growing, it swims through the deep, icy waters, going where its appetite and the currents take it. It has no special destination. As it grows from a smolt into an adult salmon, its face and jaw gradually become larger. Its scales increase in size. Its body becomes longer and more muscular, and it turns a bright silver.

Not until it approaches maturity does the salmon begin to feel an urge to go back to where it came from. It has never forgotten that it once lived in a very different place. A place not salty and not deep. A place shallow and flowing. A place of smooth rocks under cool water.

This pull to return to its home stream is an instinct every salmon is born with. The closer the salmon gets to maturity, the stronger the pull becomes. By early summer of its maturing year, the pull becomes irresistible, and the salmon begins its homeward journey. To return to its home stream to spawn is the goal of an adult salmon's life.

Steadily, it swims mile after mile over the distance it has traveled from its home stream. Along the way, the salmon feeds with greater and greater appetite. As the days and weeks go by, its muscles grow harder, its body stronger, and its purpose more and more sure. Spurred along by its natural urges, the returning salmon heads back to the stream it came from.

It can be fall, and sometimes almost winter, before a homebound salmon arrives back at the place where it entered the ocean as a smolt. Now it is fully grown and twice the size it was at the start of its return journey. Here it often rests for a

FRESHWATER STREAMS LIKE PIGEON CREEK TAKE YOUNG SALMON OUT TO SEA. ⤛

HOMEBOUND SALMON LEAP HIGH TO MAKE THEIR WAY UP A WATERFALL. ◂

while before making its way upstream. It may wait for other returning salmon, or for rain to raise the level of the creek. As it moves through the water, its silvery back glistens. Its body is fat and its muscles taut. It is at the peak of its strength.

Long ago, Pacific tribal people greeted the returning salmon with much excitement and great ceremony. How the fish found their way back through many hundreds of miles of ocean water mystified them. Some thought they were led by the gods or guided by the stars. (Today many scientists believe salmon follow the ocean currents to the coast.)

When a salmon enters fresh water, it stops eating. The fat stored in its body — and an incredibly strong will — sustain it.

A Coho salmon returning to Pigeon Creek must wait for high tide before it can enter the culvert that carries the creek water to Puget Sound. But many other home streams are much more difficult to reach. Many are great distances from any body of salt water, and some are connected to the ocean by great rivers filled with rocks, rapids, waterfalls, and dams. Returning to these home streams, a salmon must hurtle itself over anything in its way while battling the flow of water that runs against it.

When the obstacle is a dam, a salmon can often jump from one pool to another up a series of "steps," called a "fish ladder," built at the side of the dam. To get over a waterfall, salmon have been known to leap as high as eleven feet. If the first leap fails, the homebound salmon will try again. And again. And again. Some salmon lose their lives trying.

As it gets nearer to its home stream, the returning salmon passes by the outlets of many creeks and streams. The streams may seem very much alike to a human, but to a salmon each is different. The salmon can tell the difference by smelling it. Every stream has its own special smell that comes from the kind of plants, water, and rocks in it.

It is the remembered smell of its home stream that tells a salmon when its journey is over. Its nostrils quiver as it recognizes the smell. Its body quickens. At last it is home again. Where it finally comes to a stop may be only yards from its birthplace, or, in the case of the Jackson School salmon, from the spot where it was released into the creek.

But not all salmon migrating from stream to ocean will return.

Many smolt-size salmon are gobbled up almost as soon as they enter the sea. Water birds such as mergansers, kingfishers, sea gulls, and great blue herons feed on the tiny fish. Whales, seals, and sea lions eat larger salmon, as do eagles and

ALASKAN BROWN BEARS ARE EXPERTS AT FISHING. ➤

FISHERMEN HAUL A SALMON CATCH ABOARD. ❧

osprey. And the great nets of fishing boats catch them by the hundreds. Some of the salmon that return to the creeks and streams are caught by bears. Others lose their lives fighting their way upstream or trying to get past dams or to the tops of waterfalls.

Out of every one hundred salmon eggs laid, only one or two fish will survive to complete the return journey.

FEMALE SALMON LAYING EGGS ◄

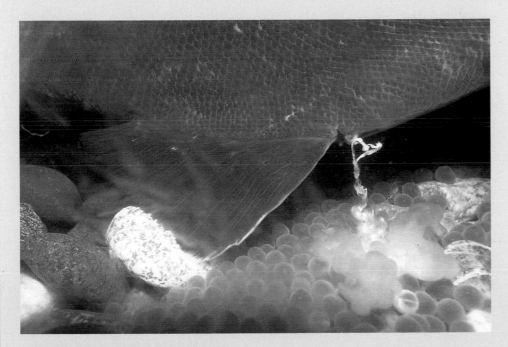

MALE SALMON FERTILIZING EGGS ◄

A NEST IS NOT ALWAYS IN A TREE

A female salmon makes her nest, or *redd,* on the gravelly bottom of a stream. Using her tail, she pounds out a long hollow twelve or more inches deep and several feet long. It has to be big enough to hold more than three thousand eggs, each the size of a pea in a pod.

As the eggs are being laid, the male salmon covers them with a milky spray called *milt,* which contains the sperm that fertilize the eggs. Producing eggs or sperm is called *spawning.*

Except for the Steelhead, which returns to the sea, Pacific salmon die soon after spawning. Their bodies become part of the stream that will feed and nourish a new generation of salmon. The young will hatch from the developing eggs, grow, migrate to the sea, and return to the same creek to spawn. Then they, too, will die — leaving another new generation of salmon to start the cycle all over again.

CHAPTER 6 ⚓

COME BACK, SALMON

JACKSON FIFTH GRADERS KEPT WATCH FOR RETURNING SALMON. ⚓

"Do you think any will come back?"

"Sure. That is, I think I'm sure."

Almost every day after school, there were students down at the creek taking a look at the little fish skittering through the water.

"When Kathi Salmon comes back to Pigeon Creek, she'll find a nice clean creek where she can lay her eggs."

"You mean, *if* she comes back."

"She will if a bigger fish doesn't eat her — "

"Or a fisherman doesn't catch her — "

"I once saw an eagle catch a salmon. They swoop down from the sky and grab it with their claws."

"Ughh."

Do you think any will come back?

The question was asked again and again. It was asked many times after the fry were released into Pigeon Creek in May 1985.

But no one knew for sure. Not even the mayor of the city of Everett. When he proclaimed the last day in May 1985 "Salmon Day" at Jackson Elementary School and Evergreen Middle School, classes celebrated the event with a picnic on the beach. But no one could be sure that any of the salmon released would ever return to Pigeon Creek.

When school started again in September, a plexiglass aquarium bought with another grant replaced the glass tank in the wall between the hallway and Mrs. Hill's first grade room. Continuous fresh water came through a tube leading from the sink. An improved filter system kept the incoming water clean, and a thermostat regulated the temperature automatically. No longer did the tank bottom have to be cleaned or the water changed by hand.

The new aquarium was stocked with four hundred eggs instead of a thousand. Caring for them was easier now. It took only a few hours a week.

CHILDREN OFTEN CHECKED THE CULVERT THAT FISH WOULD COME THROUGH TO ENTER PIGEON CREEK. ❧

FIRST GRADERS INSPECTED THE NEW TANK AND FILTER SYSTEM. ◄

The incoming first graders shared their classroom with a new batch of eyed eggs in the fish tank. The new second and third graders continued to be frequent visitors. The new fourth graders took over the twice-a-day feeding. The new fifth graders took over the daily job of water testing. The former fifth graders, now at Evergreen Middle School, came back every week to help keep their adopted stream clean.

In May 1986, the new batch of fry was released into Pigeon Creek. By then, Kathi, Jayne, Harlan Q. Hudpucker, and others of the first batch had grown into smolts. They had left the creek and were on their way downstream into Puget Sound.

A year later, in May 1987, another new batch of fry was released. It was time for Harlan Q. Hudpucker and the others, somewhere out in the Pacific Ocean, to begin their journey home.

Do you think any will come back?

The new fifth graders started to watch for returning salmon as soon as school began again after the summer vacation. One or two patrolled the banks of the stream almost every day before or after school and on Saturdays and Sundays. They walked up and down the banks of Pigeon Creek, peering into the flowing water. They crossed the railroad tracks to look into the culvert that carried the creek water into Puget Sound.

"What's that?"

"Where?"

"Over there. See?"

"That's nothing but a piece of wood."

"For a minute I thought it was a fish."

"My mother says it's more than likely that none will ever come back."

"Well, she could be wrong."

"My dad says it'll be a miracle if any come back."

"I'm going to keep looking anyway."

Some students kept on looking all through September and October. They didn't stop looking even when the rains began.

One wet November morning, rain splattered against the windows of the red brick school on top of the hill. Water filled the gutters and ran down street drains. Children in red boots and yellow slickers sloshed through mud puddles on their way to school. The smell of wet wool sweaters and plastic rain gear hung over the school hallways. Every time the entry doors opened, a flurry of wet drops flew through them.

It was still raining when Ryan Smith burst into his fifth grade classroom. "Mr. King, Mr. King," he shouted to his teacher. "I saw a fish in Pigeon Creek!"

Screeches of excitement bounced around the room. Mr. King grabbed his raincoat, and he and Mr. Baker dashed out of the school building.

There, resting on the gravelly bottom of Pigeon Creek, was an adult male Coho salmon. Nearly all its silvery color was gone. Its sides were bright red, and its

RETURNED SALMON DISPLAYED THEIR SPAWNING COLORS.

A SALMON'S SCALES TELL ITS AGE

The salmon has a coat made of scales. These scales cover the fish from its head to its tail, overlapping each other like shingles on a roof. Though the scales are thin and soft, they are made of a kind of bone and offer protection for the skin. A slimy covering over the scales adds more protection and helps the fish slide easily through the water. It also helps keep off fungi and bacteria.

As the salmon grows, its scales grow, too. You can tell how old a salmon is by examining a scale. Each has rings like the ones you see on a cut end of a tree trunk. These rings are called *circuli.* Some rings are close together, and some are farther apart. The rings that are farther apart show growth in the warm summer months, when the salmon is more active and eats more. The rings that are closer together show the growth in winter, when the salmon eats less and grows less. Each band of winter rings, called an *annulus,* counts one full year of the salmon's life.

ANNULUS

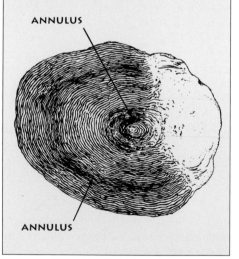

ANNULUS

SPARKLING CLEAR PIGEON CREEK WELCOMED THE SALMON HOME. ❧

back and head were bluish green. Its jaw, with its strongly hooked teeth, was almost fierce-looking. Nearby, flipping their tails gently in the clear, flowing water of the stream, were two more returned salmon. These were females, and their color was less brilliant.

"They came back! They came back!" students were shouting all over the school.

The news flew through the city of Everett and beyond. The first of the Coho salmon raised from eyed eggs in a Jackson Elementary School room and released two years before into Pigeon Creek had returned! In the next few days, ten more salmon made their way back. As they spawned, the rain fell on the clean waters of Pigeon Creek and on the awed faces of those who came to see.

No fish had returned to Pigeon Creek to spawn for more than twenty years.

In the weeks and months that followed, the return of the salmon was featured in newspapers and magazines throughout the country, and on the PBS television series "Nova." Cleaning up polluted streams and bringing fish back to them was no longer an impossible dream. Children in a little school in Everett had done it.

An ABC television crew came to Jackson School just in time to film the return of twenty-three salmon the next year. And a delegation of Japanese grade school students, who had adopted a river in Japan, arrived soon after to share ideas.

The pictures and stories in the newspapers, the programs on television, and the visitors to Pigeon Creek delighted the people in the city of Everett. But what really mattered to the children of Jackson School was that the salmon had come back.

JACKSON STUDENTS SHARED THEIR WATER-TESTING METHODS WITH VISITORS FROM JAPAN. ➤

GLOSSARY

Alevin

A newly hatched salmon with its yolk sac still attached.

Embryo

The tiny living thing inside a fertilized egg.

Environment

Everything surrounding a living thing that affects the way it grows or develops.

Eyed egg

A month-old egg at the stage when the embryo's large, dark eyes can be seen through the egg membrane.

Fertilize

To combine sperm with an egg to create new life.

Fish ladder

A series of pools arranged like steps, so a fish can jump up from one to the next.

Fry

Baby salmon that have used up their yolk sacs and are ready to find their own food.

Gill

The organ that fish use for breathing.

Hatch

To come forth from an egg.

Milt

Sperm-filled fluid sprayed by a male fish to fertilize eggs.

Plankton

Tiny organisms that float or drift in the sea.

Pollution

Whatever poisons or destroys the cleanliness and purity of air, earth, or water.

Redd

The hole (nest) in the bottom of a stream in which a female salmon lays her eggs.

Salmonid

The *Salmonidae* family, which includes salmon, trout, chars, and whitefish.

Smolt

A young salmon that is ready to migrate to the ocean.

Spawn

To lay eggs or fertilize them.

Species

A type, or kind, of plant or animal.

Sperm

The seed of life in a male.

Watershed

The drainage area around a stream or river.

Yolk sac

The food supply that is attached to the baby salmon when it hatches.

INDEX